THE WORLD OF
CHIEF SEATTLE

THE WORLD OF CHIEF SEATTLE

How Can One Sell the Air?

Warren Jefferson

Native Voices
Book Publishing Co.
Summertown, Tennessee

© 2001 Warren Jefferson

Cover and interior design: Warren Jefferson

Published in the United States by:

Native Voices, an imprint of Book Publishing Co.
P.O. Box 99
Summertown, TN 38483
888-260-8458
http://www.bookpubco.com

07 06 05 04   2 3 4 5

Printed in Canada

Photographs from the Suquamish Tribal Archives and excerpts from the Suquamish Tribal Oral History Project are used with permission of the Suquamish Tribe. Copyright the Suquamish Museum

ISBN: 1-57067-095-1

Cover photo: *Evening on Puget Sound*, by E.S. Curtis, c. 1899. Special collections, University of Washington library, #080. STA 1106.

Jefferson, Warren, 1943-
      The world of Chief Seattle: how can one sell the air? / Warren Jefferson
            p. cm.
      Includes bibliographical references
      ISBN 1-57067-095-1 (pbk. : alk. paper)
        1. Suquamish Indians--History. 2. Suquamish Indians--Social life and customs. 3. Seattle, Chief, 1790-1866--Oratory. 4. Speeches, addresses, etc., Suquamish. I. Title.

E99.S85 J43 2001
979.7004'979--dc21

                                                                    00-062463

When the sea is out, the table is set. —Puget Salish saying

TABLE OF CONTENTS

Photographs

ILLUSTRATIONS

The following illustrations are by the author.

The following illustrations are by other artists.

THE ILLUSTRATIONS IN THIS BOOK, EXCEPT MOSQUITO MASK DANCER PAGE 111, ARE AVAILABLE FOR PURCHASE BY CONTACTING THE PUBLISHER:

BOOK PUBLISHING CO.
P. O. BOX 99
SUMMERTOWN, TN 38483
931-964-3571

PREFACE

Lawrence Webster was a retired logger, like thousands of men in northwest Washington. However, Webb, as he was known, was a member of a small and special group. He was an Elder of the Suquamish Tribe and a speaker of the Puget Sound Salish language. Born in 1899, Webb was a former Tribal Chairman and lived in Indianola, near where he was raised. The sidebar quotes from him and other Suquamish Elders are taken from interviews given on the Port Madison Indian Reservation as part of the Suquamish Tribal Oral History Project.

Marilyn Jones is Director of the Suquamish Museum and an Oral Historian for the Suquamish Tribe. She was born and raised on the Port Madison Indian Reservation, and as a young girl began a lifelong quest to learn about the traditional ways of her tribe. At age seven she would lead tours of area students through the reservation, showing them important sites of her people and telling them stories she heard from the Elders about the "old days." She was eventually hired as an Oral Historian for the Suquamish Tribal Cultural Center's Oral History Project. The sidebar quotes from her are taken from an informal interview by the author on the Port Madison Indian Reservation on April 22, 1999.

I want to give a special thanks to Marilyn Jones for making available to me Suquamish Tribal archives and for her help in editing this book for accuracy according to Suquamish Tribal history.

Warren Jefferson

INTRODUCTION

This is the story of Chief Seattle and his tribe, the Suquamish. They live on Kitsap Peninsula on the shores of Puget Sound across from Seattle, Washington, in an area known as the Pacific Northwest region of the United States. The Suquamish have lived in this region for thousands of years.

Chief Seattle is renowned for a powerful and eloquent speech he gave in 1854 during treaty negotiations with agents of the United States government. In his speech, Chief Seattle expressed a commitment to living in peace with the settlers and their new culture, and he asked, in turn, that the settlers respect his people and the natural world that they shared. Today his words live on and have inspired many in the human rights and environmental movements around the world.

Before contact with non-Natives, the Suquamish were a powerful tribe in control of a large area of northern Puget Sound. Their chiefs were very influential and had extensive alliances with other tribes throughout the region. As a young man, Chief Seattle distinguished himself as an effective military leader and strategist by stopping raids by aggressive tribes from the north. Because of his military successes and great oratory ability, he became chief of both the Suquamish and the Duwamish tribes.

Chief Seattle was a young boy when European explorers first sailed into Puget Sound in 1792, nearly 300 years after Columbus "discovered" America. During the next seventy-three years, in the course of one man's lifetime, the tribes of Puget Sound went from enjoying a culturally rich, autonomous lifestyle to almost total decimation by the non-Native society.

. . . the very dust under your feet responds more lovingly to our footsteps than to yours, because it is the ashes of our ancestors, and our bare feet are conscious of the sympathetic touch, for the soil is rich with the life of our kindred. —Chief Seattle

My ancestors had built seventeen longhouses located through out their area of control. —Marilyn Jones

13

When Vancouver and my ancestors first met, it was peaceful, with mutual respect on both sides.
—Marilyn Jones

Throughout his adult life, Chief Seattle did everything he could to maintain friendly relations with the non-Native people while trying to insure that his people did not lose their land and culture. Some have said his efforts were ineffective considering the disruptive changes in lifestyle that were forced upon the Suquamish and other tribes in the region. Many died from Euro-American diseases, tribal culture and religion were suppressed, most traditional tribal lands were appropriated, and the people were confined to limited and inadequate reservations. By 1900, a rich and diverse Native culture, thousands of years old, had been brought to the brink of destruction.

But looked at another way, Chief Seattle's leadership was very important. His people never went to war with their white neighbors and the Suquamish, as a tribe, have survived to this day. Much of their culture is

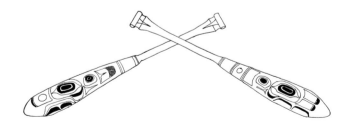

intact; they maintain sovereignty over thousands of acres along Puget Sound, and their leaders are an effective political force for Native rights in the region.

Today, Chief Seattle's spirit lives on in the hearts and minds of his people, the people of Seattle, and thousands of people around the world. His spirit returns whenever someone reads his speech, a document of grand eloquence and enduring inspiration, the testimony of a people of intelligence and sensitivity who could only hope for the best as their world came crashing down around them.

Chief Seattle is buried on Suquamish Tribal land, land that he loved and helped secure for his people. Across the sound from his grave site is the city of Seattle—a city named in honor of this great Chief.

THE LAND

Author's note: The British explorer, George Vancouver, upon first seeing this area in 1792, wrote in his diary: *The serenity of the climate, the innumerable pleasing landscapes, and the abundant fertility that unassisted nature puts forth, require only to be enriched by the industry of man.*

The Pacific Northwest region is a narrow strip of coastal land extending from the northern end of the Alaska panhandle, through coastal British Columbia south to the mouth of the Columbia River. To the west lies the Pacific Ocean and to the east the Cascade Mountains. These are volcanic mountains and there are still fissures with rising steam from some of the peaks today. Five hundred years ago, because of lava close to the surface, a side of Mt. Rainier gave way and slid into Puget Sound, creating the land on which the present city of Seattle sits.

Thousands of islands are scattered off the mainland, and in some areas in the north, fjords as dramatic and beautiful as those in Norway can be found. Lush rain forests of spruce, fir, red and yellow cedar, hemlock, and pine trees blanket the land, growing right up to the coastline. The region is interlaced with rivers, streams, and creeks of all sizes fed by fall and winter rains and by melting snow from the mountains in the spring.

Most of the region enjoys a relatively mild climate thanks in part to the Japanese current that passes along the coast. Only areas to the north in Alaska get regular freezing temperatures and heavy snowfall. The Cascade Mountains capture moisture coming off the Pacific Ocean, producing a wet climate six months of the year. Yet, surprisingly, the total rain accumulation in the Seattle area averages only 36 inches a year (New York gets 40 inches a year), and there are few torrential downpours. Most of the rain occurs during the months of October through March.

Puget Sound is located in the northwest corner of Washington State near the Canadian border. It lies between the Cascade and Olympic mountains with Mt. Baker to the north and Mt. Rainier (the highest in the range at 14,410 feet) to the south. It encompasses more than 700 square miles of waterway and 1,400 miles of coastline. Before Euro-American contact, it was the center of much Native commerce and activity all along its shores. Today Puget Sound is one of the finest harbors on the Pacific Rim and the center of the salmon industry in the Northwest.

THE PEOPLE

Since the 1930s, most archeologists held the belief that Paleo-Indians crossed the land bridge from Siberia to Alaska and began hunting in this region soon after the last Ice Age, approximately 9,000 to 13,000 years ago. But that date has been pushed back significantly. Since the 1970s, evidence has surfaced that places the date back 30,000 years before the present and possibly beyond. In the Yukon's Old Crow Basin in Alaska, a 27,000-year-old bone from a caribou was found. Microscopic evidence indicates that it was modified while still green and used to remove animal flesh from hides. (*National Geographic* magazine, September, 1979)

Anthropologists say Native People have been here for about 11,000 years. We know our people have been here since the beginning of time.

There are stories told of ancient times when ice covered our land and the people would travel through ice tunnels to visit neighboring tribes.

—Marilyn Jones

Because of geography, the people of the Pacific Northwest were somewhat isolated from inland influences and developed a culture unlike any

other in North America. At the time of Euro-American contact (beginning in 1741), in a technological sense the people were living in the Stone Age, for they had little knowledge of metal tools. There were isolated instances of tribes using metal from acquired sources like Japanese shipwrecks and inland trading, but this was the exception and not the rule. Their indigenous tools were made of bone, antler, ivory, stone, shell, and wood. But these tools were not primitive; hand-knapped flint, for instance, can be sharper than surgical steel.

They were a marine-orientated canoe society and built finely crafted dugout canoes for ocean, inlet, and river travel. The ocean, the innumerable

bays, the rivers, and the forest provided an abundant and reliable source of food and other natural products. This abundance allowed the people to develop a rich cultural life with leisure time enough to produce a plethora of beautiful art.

The favorable environmental conditions and the people's ability to gather and store food made it possible to maintain large, stable villages much like agricultural people elsewhere. But the Suquamish and other tribes here didn't farm; there was no need when food was so plentiful. Villages were situated along the sea coasts and rivers and were inhabited for many generations. An active system of trade and social exchange existed up and down the coast, extending inland as far as the Cascade Mountains. Here the people truly prospered.

Author's note: During this discussion I have been speaking in the past tense but it should be noted that many of these indigenous tribes, including the Suquamish, are still living here and maintain sovereignty over portions of their ancestral lands.

TRIBES

The indigenous people of the Pacific Northwest can be divided into three main groupings: the people of the North, the Central people, and the people of the South. Each group had their own distinct art styles, cultural traits, language, and physical characteristics. Additionally, tribes are grouped according to language. The Coast Salish (to which Chief Seattle's people, the Suquamish and Duwamish, belong) lived throughout the southern portion of the coast, lower Vancouver Island, and the mainland; the Nootka lived on the west coast of Vancover Island; the Makah, Quileute, and Quinault lived on the Olympic Peninsula at Cape Flattery; the Kwakiutl made their home on the northeastern portions of Vancouver Island around Queen Charlotte Strait and the adjacent mainland; and the Bella Coola lived on the central coast of British Columbia. Further north, the Tsimshian lived along the lower reaches of the Nass and Skeena Rivers; the Haida lived on the Queen Charlotte Islands; and further north still were the Tlingit Indians living along the fjords and islands of the panhandle of Alaska. This region was the most linguistically diverse area outside of California.

Tribes here did not organize into large political units. Of course, there were trade alliances among various tribes and loose knit alliances among villages for mutual defense, but there were no great nations as with the Plains tribes or the Iroquois Confederacy.

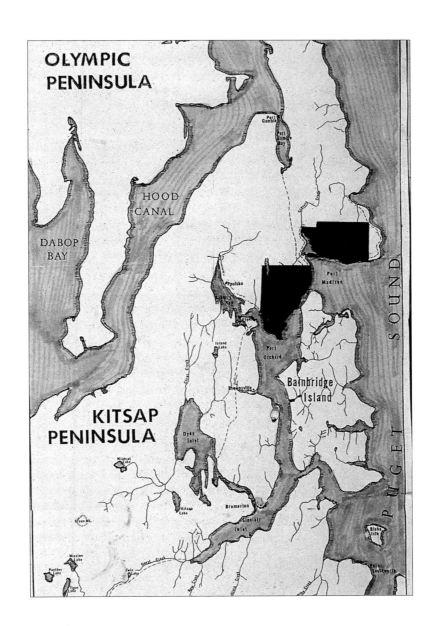

OLYMPIC
PENINSULA

HOOD
CANAL

DABOP
BAY

Port
Gamble

Port
Gamble
Bay

Poulsbo

Port
Madison

Island
Lake

Port
Orchard

Bainbridge
Island

KITSAP
PENINSULA

Dyes
Inlet

Wildcat
Lake

Brownsville

Kitsap
Lake

Green Mt.

Bremerton

Sinclair
Inlet

Blake
Island

Mission
Lake

Panther
Lake

Twin
Lakes

Point
Southworth

Tiger
Lake

P U G E T   S O U N D

25

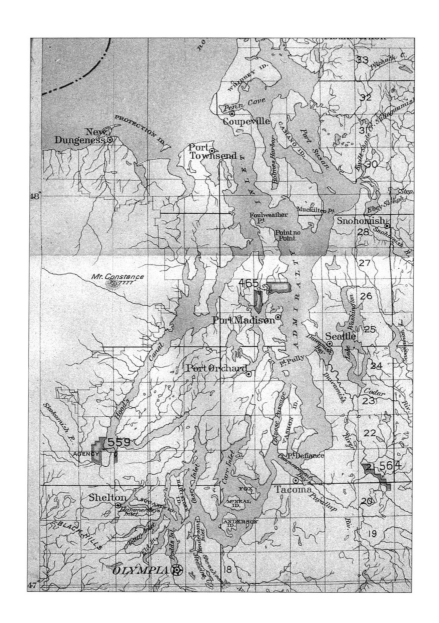

COMMERCE BETWEEN TRIBES

Tribes up and down the coast had frequent interaction with each other. They came together to maintain alliances, exchange trade goods, and to attend potlatches. Tribes in Alaska traveled to California to trade, and in the Haida oral tradition they tell of voyages to Hawaii!

The Suquamish traded from Alaska to Northern California and into Montana. —Marilyn Jones

The Suquamish Tribe of Puget Sound participated in an extensive network of alliances before Euro-American contact. The alliances made among tribes were secured through marriage. In addition to mutual defense, tribes obtained economic benefits from trade and the exchange of ideas. Food baskets, mats, blankets, canoes, and raw materials were basic to the economic structure of the area. Each group had an overabundance of specific commodities for trade: the Suquamish had dried clams, the Makah had whale products, and the Snohomish had deer or bear meat. (The Suquamish Museum, 1985)

SOCIAL SYSTEM

Suquamish society at this time was communal in nature with fishing and hunting areas shared freely among tribal members. People took care of each other. Even today the people of my generation consider that we are brothers and sisters. —Marilyn Jones

In most tribes there existed a highly developed social system composed of a hereditary aristocracy, common people, and slaves. This system was not rigid, for a commoner could rise in standing through the accumulation of wealth or by strong actions during times of crisis. In many tribes much emphasis was placed on material wealth which was conspicuously displayed and given away during a potlatch, a ceremony unique to this region. A successful potlatch would very likely increase the host's standing among his peers.

Family ties were very important and lineage was tracked closely. Each family belonged to a clan with each clan having the right to perform special dances and songs and, in some tribes, the exclusive use of resources in certain areas.

Since there were no written languages, the origins and history of the village and the accomplishments of ancestral leaders were remembered through oral tradition during ceremonies and the story telling of myths and legends. Art played an important role in preserving village history and in recording genealogy. Canoes were decorated with symbols of clan exploits, and the heraldic totem poles this region is noted for were used to symbolize family lineage and ranking and to record the heroic acts of ancestors.

Slavery was practiced throughout the region, but unlike slavery practiced by whites against blacks in the southern United States at this time, it was a relatively benign system. Slaves were acquired through trade or as the result of a successful attack on another village. Slaves were generally well treated and in some tribes became members of the family.

Chiefs owned slaves and slave ownership was a status symbol. Some chiefs owned as many as ten or twelve individuals. Slaves did the menial work, paddled the canoe, gathered firewood, cooked the meals, made baskets, and took care of anything else that needed to be done. They also procreated with their owners, in which case the children would be born into slavery. But in some tribes female slaves could marry free men and become free. Slavery was so prevalent that in some areas one-tenth of the population was in bondage.

In reality, there were no hereditary chiefs among the Puget Sound tribes. Strong leaders arose in each village from time to time who, distinguishing themselves by their actions or particular skills, were respected and followed. For instance, there were fishing leaders, peacetime leaders, and leaders in times of crisis. [Chief] Seattle was one of these. [A leader in times of crisis] (The Suquamish Museum, 1985)

Slaves would not try to escape. It was a dishonor to run away. Slaves could return home if their relatives or tribe traded something of equal value for them. —Marilyn Jones

POTLATCH

The word potlatch means "gift" or "to give" in Chinook jargon, a common language of the region in the 1800s. It was an important event put on by all chiefs to ensure their position or to increase standing.

A potlatch would be held to mark any important event: a marriage, the birth of a child or naming ceremony for a child, the coming of age of a daughter or son, or a death in the family. They were sponsored by one person, or a

group of people could hold one together. They were usually held in the fall or winter so as not to interfere with food-gathering activities.

The value and quantity of the gifts given away and the amount of food consumed would determine the success of the potlatch. A grand potlatch could last for three weeks and include more than 1,000 people coming from as far as 100 miles to attend. A successful potlatch would be remembered for years and the host talked about as a most generous leader.

> The Ole Man house, where he [Chief Seattle] resided, was a famous gathering place for the natives from all over the Sound, and some of the potlatches held there have been attended by as many as 8,000 Indians. I saw one there at which there was fully 1,500 present. (Coombs, 1893)

Feasting and gambling would go on throughout the days, while the nights would be spent dancing and singing and in religious ceremonies. It was a good time for socializing and finding a wife or husband. During the "give away," which was usually the last event of the celebration, silver and gold coins would be passed out and canoes, blankets, guns and ammunition, robes, baskets, utensils, shell and bead work, and other items of value would be given away.

The value of the gifts could total more than $3,000 (valued in nineteenth century dollars). Potlatches were outlawed in the early 1900s in an effort to suppress Native culture and force assimilation of the Native people.

It is difficult to accurately establish the population of this region before the arrival of non-Native people, but some estimates suggest there were some 150,000 people living in one 176,000 square mile area alone. In 1835 there were estimates of 47,000 Native people living in coastal British Columbia, and the Coast Salish were thought to number 12,000. The Suquamish tribe at that time numbered around 5,000 members.

Intertribal Warfare

There was constant intertribal warfare among the warlike tribes but the fighting was more like skirmishes than true warfare. There were very few pitched battles engaging large numbers of warriors. More commonly there were raids and counter-raids and revenge killings that would go on for generations.

Typically a war party would arrive by canoe at night to raid and plunder a village. There would be a fight, and the men would either successfully defend the village or were killed or run off. Any women and children captured would become slaves. The taking of heads by the victors was commonplace. Taken back to the village they were displayed as war trophies in front of the homes of the fighters. With the introduction of firearms by traders, the fighting intensified and, tragically, whole villages were sometimes destroyed.

The Suquamish and other tribes of Puget Sound were often the victims of raids by tribes from the north, such as the Haida and Tsimshian. Chief Seattle gained much of his authority in the region because of his ability to organize the Puget Sound tribes and successfully defend against such attacks.

FOOD

Food was plentiful throughout the region. From the sea, the people would harvest fish and shellfish. Bi-yearly salmon runs offered the most reliable source of food. Vast amounts were harvested and smoked to last through the year. Marine animals such as sea otters, seals, and whales, as well as water fowl, were taken as the animals migrated into local waters.

Clams were an important food and were dug on a year-round basis, providing a constant supply of fresh food. Even in the winter, when the lowest tides were at night, clams were dug using torches of cedar bark and pitchwood. In spring, large quantities of littleneck clams, cockles, and horse clams were harvested and dried for later use or traded.

You want to leave things as they are and just take what you need. Don't be wasteful, that's what the Elders taught. —Martha George

While the men fished and hunted, women dried and smoked fish and shellfish for winter storage. To supplement their diet, women and children also gathered a variety of plants including thimbleberry sprouts, salmonberries, elderberries, cranberries, marsh tea and Indian potatoes. Plants were also used as medicines and in the making of baskets and mats. (Suquamish Museum, 1985)

Around these creeks when the salmon come in the fall and they'd gather up in front, you'd swear you could walk on 'em. All these creeks had salmon in them. Now there's very few that do.
—Lawrence Webster

From the forest, hunters took black bear, deer, elk, mountain goat, rabbit, and beaver. Insects and a wide variety of plants, roots, and berries were collected as well. For thousands of years the indigenous people of this region efficiently exploited these resources, yet they lived in balance with the natural world, taking only what they needed.

HOUSES

During the wet winter months, extended families lived together in communal longhouses. Some were quite large and could be home for 100 people. Chief Seattle and his extended family lived in the largest longhouse on Puget Sound—reportedly 700 feet long and 60 feet wide! It was 15 feet high in the front and 10 feet high in the rear. When explorers first saw these longhouses, they were amazed that the buildings could be constructed without the use of metal tools.

The longhouse was a solid structure built of cedar. Cedar is a soft wood with straight grain that allows it to be easily worked into planks and beams. (Planks four feet wide and forty feet long have been noted by some historians.)

Trees for the house were felled using stone adzes (traditionally, jadeite or nephrite) and fire. Once on the ground, branches were removed and the logs were cut to size. These were then either used for poles or split into beams and planks using antler or wood wedges and stone malls.

To begin the building process, the main support poles were set into the ground along the perimeter of the house. Cross beams were secured to the top of the poles to tie the structure together and support the roof. This stage of building required an enormous amount of effort, as these poles were large and quite heavy. The walls were fashioned with planks that were set vertically into the ground and secured to the top beams with flexible cedar branches or stacked horizontally on top of each other and tied to the poles. Cracks were chinked with moss, and the interior wall was covered with woven mats. Roof planks were ingeniously fashioned with grooves and flanges that interlocked to keep the rain out.

In the front there was an opening that was secured during inclement weather by a rough door laid over the opening and held in place by a brace. A smaller opening in the rear of the house allowed exit from that side. There were no windows.

The Suquamish Tribe was building a longhouse and they were having trouble getting this one large beam lifted into place. They tried and tried but could not do it. They were very frustrated.

So they decided to have a potlatch. They feasted and shared with everyone and then as a challenge they asked each visiting tribe to lift this log into place. Each tribe tried but none could do it. So the host tribe took their turn and this time were successful.

The other tribes teased them saying you just wanted to show off. But really they just needed that extra encouragement to get the job done.
—Marilyn Jones as told to her by
Tribal Elders

Running the length of the house down the center was a wide trench about a foot in depth in which the cooking fires were tended. Smoke from the fires was vented out the roof through spaces that could be opened and closed by moving special roof boards.

Along the walls were sleeping platforms, and in some houses there were double bunks built one over another. Under the platform, personal items were stowed or the slaves slept. Woven mat partitions were used to separate families and provide a level of privacy. All in all, these houses were very substantial structures that adequately protected the occupants from the elements.

In the spring and summer these longhouses were empty, for the people had moved on to summer hunting and gathering areas. Here they lived in temporary houses made of woven cattail mats and light framing which could be easily moved from place to place as needed.

CLOTHING

The people of the southern region (which includes the Coast Salish) enjoyed a relatively mild climate, so everyday clothing before contact with Euro-Americans was minimal for both men and women. Very often in warm weather the women went topless and the men wore nothing at all.

Traditional clothing during colder weather was usually shredded cedar bark garments. Men wore tunics of woven cedar bark edged with fur to reduce the roughness, while women wore a simple cedar apron tied at the back. Over this apron the women could wear a knee-length wraparound garmet of woven cedar bark or a tunic similar to the men. Capes of shredded cedar bark, conical in shape and waist-length, were worn, as well as cedar-bark blankets and Salish wool blankets. Most people went barefoot all year.

The noble class wore fur and skin robes. Sea otter robes were the most prized, along with bear robes, and were worn during important occasions. At other times marten, seal, raccoon, and bobcat furs were worn.

A basketry hat was worn for protection from the sun and rain. Made from splints of cedar roots and hemp fiber and woven together very tightly, it was quite waterproof. Shaped like an inverted bowl, it was about fifteen inches wide at the brim and often embellished with graphic designs woven in during construction. In the winter, men and women wore fur caps. (Paterek, 1994)

By 1860 most Puget Sound natives had adopted the dress of Euro-American settlers. Photos from the era show men wearing trousers, vests, bowler hats, cotton shirts, suspenders, and shoes or boots. The women are wearing long dresses or skirt-and-blouse combinations with shawls and head-scarves, and shoes or boots.

William We-oh-lup

THE CANOE

As the horse was to the Plains People and the dog sled to the Eskimo, so the canoe was to the people of the Pacific Northwest. The coastline here is rocky and heavily forested, making land travel difficult at best. The canoe allowed travel to summer hunting and fishing grounds and efficient transport of people and goods over long distances.

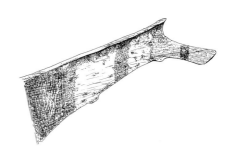

These superbly crafted dugout canoes were beautiful vessels with graceful, curving lines and smooth, well-finished hulls. Canoes were of various sizes depending upon use. Larger ones were fifty feet long and eight feet wide and could carry as much as six to eight tons—some could seat thirty people. The Haida and Makah people were noted for their ocean-going canoes, fashioned with high bows and sterns to cut through the waves. Some canoes were fitted with sails of cedar bark, and later, canvas.

After being neglected for several generations canoes are again being built by many tribes in the region. Tribal leaders have come to realize that the canoe is an important connection to the past and a powerful symbol of Native identity.

In 1989 a flotilla of more than thirty canoes from throughout the region traveled or *pulled* to Seattle during Washington State's Centennial Celebration. This canoe journey, called a *paddle*, showed the participating tribes the power of the canoe journey to unify and instill tribal pride. This Centennial paddle marked the beginning of the resurgence of the canoeing tradition. Since then, annual canoe races and paddles have been held up and down the coast, and yearly canoe journeys to initiate young people into adulthood have been taking place in many tribes.

In 1993 the Suquamish Traditional Canoe Society was formed to help revive the West Coast Salish canoe culture. Since then the Society has joined other Northwest tribes in making an annual canoe journey to various locations throughout western Washington and Canada. Many of these journeys involve hundreds of miles of water travel over many days and nights.

Traditionally canoes and canoe building had a spiritual dimension, and in some tribes the builder practiced a highly elaborate ritual of purification and prayer before and during the carving. It was a highly prized skill that took many years to master.

I want to see the canoes again
I need to feel the rain on my face
And wipe the drops from my eyes
Hug my drum under my jacket
Sing with Lela May
Wake up in the tent
Break camp
Find the next beach.
I would like to stand on the sand
With all the other Tribes
And watch, proud
And full of understanding
As the canoes
Once again bring to us
Our culture
Our future

Our dignity.
Look, get your songs ready
See the canoes come
Around the point!
Again.
This is our ancestors
And our future.
Sing out with pride
Again.

—Peg Deam, Suquamish

The first step in the building of a canoe was to locate a suitable tree—it had to be growing near water and have a soft place to fall. For moderate size canoes only half the log, split horizontally, was used. For larger canoes, like the war canoe or cargo canoe, a whole log from a 400- to 800-year-old tree was needed.

The best canoes were traditionally constructed from red or yellow cedar. Once down, the log was cut to length, shaped to a rough form, and floated back to the village to be finished. Here the log was shaped with a stone adze and hollowed out with fire and adze. (After Euro-American contact, metal adzes were used.)

When the shape was right, the canoe was filled with water and hot rocks and covered with cattail mats until the wood became pliable enough to be spread to the proper shape. In order for the wood not to split during this process, the sides and bottom had to be quite thin. A midsize canoe 44 feet

45

long was ¾ inch thick on the sides and 1½ inch thick at the keel. Spreading a log in this fashion was quite effective. A log three feet in diameter could be spread to four feet with this method. The total process, from locating a tree to a finished canoe, could take up to a year to complete. (Lincoln, 1991)

> The [canoe] journey is a ceremony. The canoe journey is very spiritual. Every motion in the universe has an equal and opposite force. This is a law of physics and a law of spirituality. When we put our canoes in the water, we made a motion in the universe. Before the canoe ever touched the water to initiate that first motion, there was thought. First we think, then we say, and then we do. The ceremony was created from thought, from a dream or vision the Creator put in our minds. Then the thought became words, then action. (Lugwub, *Suquamish Newsletter*, February, 1997)

In some tribes, chiefs and prominent people were given a canoe burial when they died. The deceased would be wrapped in robes and laid to rest in the bottom of the canoe along with personal effects that they had used during their lifetime—weapons would be put with a warrior or household items with a woman. The canoe was then covered with boards and mats to keep out scavengers and placed on a structure of posts and beams or in the boughs of a tree. After a year the body was removed and put in a cave or taken out to open water and buried at sea. Chief Seattle's grave site has two symbolic burial canoes supported on a large post and beam structure over his head stone.

Arts & Crafts

ART

Pacific Northwest art was distinct and highly developed long before Euro-American contact. Three different types of art were produced: painting, engraving and woodcarving, and weaving and basketry. Men carved and painted, and women did the weaving and basket making.

The style of carving and painting is unique to this region. It was traditionally very decorative with symbolic motifs of heraldic significance. Spectacular crests and masks were created for display or used in dances. In paintings and carvings very often animals were represented. They were depicted in stylized forms in which the vital internal organs are shown in a sort of x-ray fashion. Houses, canoes, and totem poles were carved and painted with these stylized designs, representing the creatures the tribe shared their world with. Utilitarian objects like spoons, bowls, wooden boxes for holding possessions, and many other objects were richly decorated. Art for these Native people was part of daily life; they lived within their art.

When Captain Cook came to this region in 1778, he collected many fine examples of this art which are housed today in the British Museum. And there are many fine examples of art from this period of first contact in other museums and private collections around the world.

The production of most art died out as a result of the disruption of tribal life during the end of the 1800s. But today, Native artists are reviving the old art forms and blending them with contemporary styles, producing beautiful art of value both to the collector and the preservation of tribal culture.

49

WEAVING

The weaving of the Coast Salish and their neighbors is unique in that they were the only Native people in North America to weave with wool before Euro-American contact. Salish women produced beautiful blankets with intricate geometric patterns and designs from a simple loom. They also produced baskets, mats, hats, and capes from various plant fibers.

Weaving was done by hand, no shuttle was used and rarely was a heddle used. Elders who taught the craft, thought it unwise to depend upon too many tools, when your hands could do the precise work alone. (The Suquamish Museum, 1985)

Wool for weaving blankets was collected from mountain goats and a special breed of dog now extinct. The dogs were small animals that grew long, thick coats of fine fur. Their fur grew quickly and could be shorn two or three times a year, thus the owner was assured a steady supply of high-quality wool. These dogs were highly prized by their owners and kept on separate islands so as not to interbreed with common camp dogs.

To create texture and extend the wool, the weaver would add goose and duck down and filler material from various plants. Stinging nettle fiber, fluff from the fireweed plant, Indian hemp, shredded cedar bark, and catkins from the cattail plant were all used.

Dyeing would be accomplished with red from the bark of the alder tree, yellow from lichen, brown from the bark of the hemlock tree, yellow-green from the Oregon grape, and blue-green from oxidized copper ore. Black was achieved by burying the fibers in iron-rich mud for a period of time.

Traditional weaving died out when the Hudson Bay Company introduced mass-produced blankets, but since the 1970s there has been a revival of the old weaving techniques, and superb blankets are again being produced.

BASKETRY

It was my grandmother that taught me how to make baskets. She used to go out and get the cattails and go get the cedar bark and get cedar limbs to make clam baskets. She use to make me sit down and do it. She says, 'You got to learn how. You're goin' to get old, too, like I am, so you better learn how to make this.' —Ethel Sam

Pottery was not produced by the Native people of this region, as the clay deposits here were unsuitable for making pottery. Instead they produced wonderful baskets that are highly prized today. Baskets that have survived from the 1800s bring thousands of dollars on the auction market. Baskets made by the Coast Salish were famous for their beauty and functionality.

The complicated system of harvest, transport, and storage [of food and other items] required making a great variety of baskets, each with a special use. Baskets were also woven as beautiful objects to be admired and given away to friends and relatives. Many were made specifically for trade with other tribes, or for sale as non-Native people came to the area. Most basket making was done by women.

The coiled, or hard, basket was the most versatile of all containers made, and was considered the most valuable. It was used when picking berries, for carrying liquids, for storing dried foods, and for cooking. The open weave, twine "clam baskets" were useful for gathering clams, small fish, or seaweed. Roots and limbs of cedar were split into narrow strips to supply the raw material for such baskets. In coiled baskets some of these strips became the foundation for the wide horizontal coil, while others were used to sew the coil together with the aid of a sharp bone awl. Small strips of colored plant material, such as wild cherry bark, horsetail root, or dyed cedar bark, were sometimes folded under each stitch. This technique, known as imbrication, produced geometric patterns on the baskets. Twined baskets were made with a vertical warp of twisted cattail fibers and two double-weft strands of both cattail and bear grass or some other decorative element.

Twined baskets could be so tightly sewn that when swollen by soaking in water they could become quite water tight.

The clam basket was used to gather and transport small fish, shellfish, and other "beach" foods back to the village or camp. Since the Suquamish spent almost their entire life on Puget Sound or on the adjacent tide lines, the clam basket was the most commonly used basket.

On my basket work, I was just a little girl about seven years old when I first started to work. . . any waste, little work of my mother what she would throw away, I would pick up—just a little girl. I thought I had enough and I went outside and started work on it, started at the bottom. I made a little basket. From that time I kept on working and I'm still workin' on baskets. —Celia Jackson

In making the clam basket, cedar root and cedar limbs were the most commonly used materials, although hemlock and spruce were sometimes utilized. Long, straight limbs and roots were most desirable. The best cedar roots were dug from trees growing on rotten logs, while the best limbs were taken in swampy areas. Both materials were split into sections, and the limbs were used for the main frame (warp) of the basket, while the root sections were used for wrapping (weft) to hold the basket together. Clam baskets were heavily used, and were usually discarded after one season. (The Suquamish Museum, 1985)

FIRST CONTACT

The mid- to late-1700s was the beginning of European contact for these indigenous people, almost 300 years after east coast Native people first encountered them. The first written record of contact was in 1741 between a tribe in Alaska and a group of Russian explorers. In 1772, Spanish explorers landed on the Olympic Peninsula to lay claim for Spain. They were driven away by warriors of the Makah people who still live on the northern portion of the peninsula and believe they have claim to this area since the beginning of time.

In 1778, Captain James Cook sailed through these waters with William Bligh (later of H.M.S. *Bounty* fame) and George Vancouver as junior officers. One of the many places Cook explored was Nootka Sound, off Vancouver Island. While there he wrote in his log: "A great many canoes filled with the Natives were about the ships all day, and a trade commenced betwixt us and them, which was carried on with the strictest honesty on both sides. Their articles were the skins of various animals, such as bears, wolves, foxes, deer, raccoons, polecats, martins and in particular the sea beaver, the same as is found on the coast of Kamtchatka."

Captain Vancouver returned to this area with his own ship *Discovery* in 1792. He sailed into Puget Sound to map the territory and claim the area for Britain. In 1805 Lewis and Clark explored the lower reaches of the Columbia River and claimed that region for the United States. And so this beautiful area of the country with its unimaginably rich resources was finally "discovered." Thus began the destruction of the indigenous Native culture.

TRADE WITH NON-NATIVES

During initial contact with Native people, explorers noticed their luxurious fur capes and hats. Inquiring, they learned it was from the sea otter, an animal with the softest and thickest coat of all fur animals. Captain Cook discovered that merchants in China would pay high prices for such pelts. There soon developed an active maritime fur trade, as agents of the Hudson Bay Company of Great Britain arrived to exploit this valuable resource.

The Native people were eager to trade. For their furs they could get iron blades, guns, blankets, and food stuffs that the Euro-Americans offered. It wasn't long before the Pacific Fur Company of the United States set up trading forts and began to compete with Great Britain for control of this lucrative trade. The Pacific Northwest quickly became a major center supplying furs to Asia, Europe, and cities of the eastern United States. Great fortunes were made, for in those days a bail of sea otter pelts could bring as much as $10,000.

The fur economy continued for more than twenty-five years and created much wealth. Among Native people this wealth stimulated cultural and artistic activity, and many fur trading tribes were able to support full-time artists. In the span of three years, between 1799 and 1802, more than 48,000 sea otter pelts were taken. For the next eighteen years the sea otter was relentlessly hunted. By 1820, the animal was close to extinction and the fur trade collapsed.

Author's note: The Fur Seal Treaty of 1911 saved the otter from extinction, and today they number more than 120,000.

57

By the middle of the nineteenth century, this region was experiencing tremendous change. Along with trade items, non-Native people brought diseases such as smallpox and cholera, to which the indigenous population had no resistance. Whole villages were wiped out, and in some areas populations were reduced by as much as ninety percent. The first epidemic of smallpox struck Puget Sound in 1830 and claimed many victims.

In 1841 Canada and the United States settled their border dispute, and the new boundary was marked on the 49th parallel. On January 24th, 1848, James W. Marshall discovered gold at Sutter's Mill in Coloma, California. In the short span of five years, California was transformed from a sparsely populated Mexican province into a multinational melting pot of tens of thousands of people. (Nunis, 1993) This expanding population needed vast amounts of supplies, and because of its abundant natural resources, the northwest again became an active trading center. Canneries were located up and down the coast to exploit the rich fish and shellfish resources, and a thriving lumber industry developed.

By the 1850s the American westward migration was well under way, pushed by a depression and expanding populations back east. An effort by the Federal government to "induce settlements on the public domain in distant or dangerous portions of the nation" resulted in The Oregon Donation Land Act of 1850. This act of Congress allowed new settler families to claim up to 320 acres of land and allowed those already in the region to claim 640 acres. This was before any treaties were made with the Native people of the region.

Surveys were being conducted in the region to locate the best route for a railway line to connect with cities east of the Rocky Mountains. In 1853 Washington Territory, once part of Oregon, was established. Gold was discovered in eastern Washington in 1855 and a few years later in British Columbia, causing an influx of more people.

The region very soon had a growing population competing with Native people for land and other resources. One estimate in the 1850s puts the population of the territory at 5,000 settlers, all looking for the best places to settle.

Like other tribes before them, the Native people here were treated with little regard for their natural rights. Manifest destiny, an ostensibly benevolent policy of imperialistic expansion practiced by the U. S. government at the time, was the operating principal and justification for this exploitation.

In 1850, a federal law was passed authorizing the removal and relocation of all the Northwest tribes from their homelands to an area east of the Cascades. Fortunately this law was never acted upon, and many tribes were able to stay in their accustomed areas when the treaties were ratified. Chief Seattle didn't know of these and other plans for relocation by the federal government when he spoke to a group of American settlers:

> My name is Sealth and this great swarm of people that you see are my people; they have come down here to celebrate the coming of the first run of good salmon. As the salmon are our chief food we always rejoice to see them coming early and in abundance, for this insures us a plentiful quantity of food for the coming winter. This is the reason our hearts are glad today, and so you do not want to take this wild demonstration as warlike. It is meant in the nature of a salute in imitation of the Hudson Bay Company's salute to their chiefs when they arrive at Victoria. I am glad to have you come to our country, for we Indians know but little and you Boston and King George men know how to do everything. We want your blankets, your guns, axes, clothing, tobacco, and all other things you make. We need all these things that you make, as we do not know how to make them, and so we welcome you to our country to make flour, sugar, and other things that we can trade for. We wonder why the Boston men should wander so far away from their home and come among so many Indians. Why are you not afraid? (Bagley papers)

THE SUQUAMISH TRIBE:
CHIEF SEATTLE'S PEOPLE

The name "Suquamish" comes from the main village site along Agate Passage between Bainbridge Island and Kitsap Peninsula. In the Lushootseed language the word is *d'suq'wub*, which means "the place of clear salt water." Before Euro-American contact, the village here was a place where many tribes came together for trade and celebration. It was later the site of Old Man House, the largest longhouse on Puget Sound and the home of Chief Seattle and his extended family. Old Man House was a major gathering place until the authorities, thinking the communal lifestyle was adding to the

Archaeological evidence shows that the Old Man House site had been continuously occupied for over 2,000 years. They have found human artifacts on that site that are 12,000 years old. . . .Our homeland before contact ran from Point No Point in the north to Gig Harbor in the south and across to areas around what is now Seattle. —Marilyn Jones

spread of diseases, ordered it destroyed around 1870.

Euro-American encroachment had a devastating effect on the Coast Salish population. The Suquamish estimate that their population was more than 5,000 people before contact. By 1857 they were reduced to 441 and by 1909 there were just 180 Suquamish left on Puget Sound. By 1910 the population of the Coast Salish group was estimated to be 9,524 (Curtis, 1913) down from 12,000 before contact.

65

RELIGION

One thing [the Elders told us about spiritual power] *was you should go out and fast for about three days. If you could stay the three days and nothin' happened, you come back. And you'd have to wait awhile and try it again. And one of these times when you was out there, something was goin' to happen to you. And that is where you are going to start getting your power.* —Lawrence Webster

In ancient times, the Native peoples of Puget Sound had a living faith that was much more than a worship and respect for Nature. They saw all of existence as alive and feeling, having the same range of thoughts and emotions as human beings. The following is from contemporary Suquamish writings.

In the very beginning, there was a wonderful world here long before human beings arrived. It was a world where everything had the power and ability to take any form or do any thing. A world inhabited by beings who might appear as animals, plants, in human or inhuman form, or as aspects of the landscape, always shimmering between these and other shapes. Finally, a firm order was imposed on this world by The Changer, enabling human beings to take their place in the world.

As a result, the beings have been changed in the shapes of trees, plants, animals, fish, rocks, springs, and so forth, while their spirits retain their original abilities. In these forms they have retained their full intelligence and emotions, and many have entered into partnerships with particular individuals to grant them abilities and careers.

As the most recent inhabitants of this world, human beings are believed to have the most to learn. Yet, such an education is possible because all of life is related, forming a functioning whole. Special powers and abilities can be approached through fasting, prayer, meditation, and rituals. Many parts of the old religion are still important in the lives of those who have incorporated Catholicism, Shakerism, and other varieties of Christianity into their religious beliefs.

Traditional teachings still play an important role in the modern world. While participating in many of the same denominations as the rest of America and Europe, Native peoples have nonetheless also maintained their special relationship with the land and with its sacred aspects. As the larger population becomes more aware of the virtue of being ecumenical, ecologically aware, and respectful of the limitations of our planet, the virtues of traditional respect for nature are becoming better appreciated, understood, and encouraged. (The Suquamish Museum, 1985)

There was no Supreme Being. Only what they got from the church, but traditionally there was no Supreme Being. You come from the earth and you return to the earth.
—Lawrence Webster

CREATION OF AGATE PASS

This is a creation story of the Suquamish tribe from oral traditions handed down by the elders.

Long ago, when this land was new, the area we know as Agate Pass was much smaller than today. The people of this land could cross from one side to the other by stepping over a small body of water that it flowed into.

There lived in this larger body of water a guardian spirit, who was to protect the people and watch over them forever. This Guardian Spirit was a Giant Serpent. One day some of the women of the village were going to step across the pass to what we now call Bainbridge Island to dig clams, and the Giant serpent was angry and very mean. He came out of the water and began biting at the women. They dropped their baskets and ran back to the village, telling the people that the Guardian Spirit was angry and mean. Many went to see what was wrong. Serpent came and attacked the people. The people ran back to the village and prayed to the Great Spirit for help.

Chief Kitsap went to the pass and sang his spirit song and called his Spirit Power to help the people of the village. His spirit power was the Double Headed Eagle, and it came from the mountains. The Chief told the Spirit to stop the Serpent and its evil actions.

The Double Headed Eagle flew over the pass and the Giant Serpent came up very angry. The two began to fight, and the earth shook, and the water boiled. The Chief was singing his power song the entire time the battle was going on. After a long, long time the two vanished under the water, and the people were very frightened, believing that it was the end of Double Headed Eagle. Some of the people began to scream and cry until it was as loud as thunder.

Then, as if the earth was going to be swallowed by the waters, they began to boil and churn. Then, the Double Headed Eagle exploded out of the water and up into the sky with the body of the Giant Serpent in its claws.

The Double Headed Eagle flew back into the mountain and behind him was left the wide pass in which the waters flow so swift at the change of tides, they boil to this day.

CHIEF SEATTLE

Chief Seattle was born in 1786 into an aristocratic family. His father was a Suquamish chief named Schweabe. His mother, Scholitza, was the daughter of a Duwamish chief. He was married twice and had a daughter named Angeline by his first wife and a son named Jim by his second wife. He had other children but their names are not known. He died at age 81 on June 7, 1866, in Old Man House on the Port Madison Indian Reservation. He is buried at the St. Peters Church cemetery in the town of Suquamish, a few miles from where he died.

Henry A. Smith in his series "Early Reminiscences" describes Chief Seattle:

> Old Chief Seattle was the largest Indian I ever saw, and by far the noblest-looking. He stood 6 feet full in his moccasins, was broad-shouldered, deep-chested, and finely proportioned. His eyes were large, intelligent, expressive, and friendly when in repose, and faithfully mirrored the varying moods of the great soul that looked through them. He was usually solemn, silent, and dignified, but on great occasions moved among assembled multitudes like a Titan among Lilliputians, and his lightest word was law.

> When rising to speak in council or to tender advice, all eyes were turned upon him, and deep-toned, sonorous, and eloquent sentences rolled from his lips like the ceaseless thunders of cataracts flowing from exhaustless fountains and his magnificent bearing was as noble as that of the most cultivated military chieftain in command of the forces of a continent. Neither his eloquence, his dignity, or his grace were acquired. They were as native to his manhood as leaves and blossoms are to a flowering almond.

> His influence was marvelous. He might have been an emperor but all his

instincts were democratic, and he ruled his loyal subjects with kindness and paternal benignity. He was always flattered by marked attention from white men, and never so much as when seated at their tables, and on such occasions he manifested more than anywhere else the genuine instincts of a gentleman. (Smith, 1887)

There are very few written records of Chief Seattle's early life. What we know of his rise to power is based on tribal oral history and a few accounts written by early explorers. What we do know is that as a young man he distinguished himself as a great military leader and strategist by stopping raids from aggressive tribes to the north. The following is a war story told by the Suquamish about Chief Seattle. (Also see Coombs, 1893)

Suquamish elders didn't often speak directly about people who have passed on so we have little knowledge of previous leaders. —Marilyn Jones

It became known that a group of over one hundred warriors from inland tribes on the Green and White Rivers were assembling to stage raids on the Suquamish and other Puget Sound tribes. This was unwelcomed news because they had raided the region before and many people were killed or captured as slaves. So tribal leaders came together to plan a defense. Various ideas were discussed but none seemed like the right one. Chief Seattle spoke up. He was a young man and untested as a leader but he proposed a plan so brilliant that it was immediately accepted by the leaders.

The raiding tribes were known to be coming down the Green River. At a certain point in the river there was a section of rapids just downstream from a sharp bend. Here Seattle had his men fell a large tree. It was trimmed and put into position just below the surface of the river so as not to be visible from a canoe. Seattle and his men then hid in the forest to await the arrival of the raiding party.

74

Soon the raiders came streaming down the river. When their canoes hit the tree, they capsized and the men were swepted into the rapids. Many were dashed on the rocks and drowned. Those who made it to shore were dispatched with spear and arrow. As the others that followed learned of the situation they beached their canoes and ran away. The raiding party was completely routed. The people rejoiced and Seattle was honored in a great celebration that lasted many days.

Because of military successes as in the legend recounted above and his great oratory ability, Seattle quickly rose to a place of eminence and high regard among his people. In 1808, at age 22, he became chief of both the Duwamish and Suquamish tribes.

In 1838, Chief Seattle and other tribal leaders signed an agreement negotiated by officials from the Hudson Bay Company to end the widespread practice of revenge murder. By the 1840s he had changed from a war chief to a peace chief. He was known to the non-Native people as "great chief" and one of the most influential men on Puget Sound. Not long afterward he converted to Christianity through the Catholic church and took the name Noah Seathl which is the name on his tombstone along with Chief Seattle. He inaugurated regular prayer sessions among his people that were carried on well after his death.

Chief Seattle's original name is not known. Seattle is the name the settlers called him, his original name was too hard for them to pronounce. When he was baptized, his original name was not recorded by the church authorities and is lost.

76

The Point Elliott Treaty

THE ARRIVAL OF GOVERNOR ISAAC STEVENS

In 1853 the newly appointed governor of Washington Territory and Superintendent of Indian Affairs, Isaac Stevens, arrived in the Puget Sound area. In 1854 he was ordered to make treaties with all Indian tribes in the territory, thereby extinguishing Indian claims to these lands. Stevens was an ambitious man and saw an opportunity to make his fortune in this new land by opening a rail route to the Pacific. A biographer writes "his temperament, training, and professional career best prepared him to operate as a monarch." (Richards, 1993)

He was a firm believer in manifest destiny and held the bizarre view that the Native people of this region welcomed the disintegration of their culture. In a report to the Bureau of Indian Affairs he wrote, "The speedy extinction of the race seems rather to be hoped for than regretted, and they look forward to it themselves with a sort of indifference." (Stevens, 1854, 453.) Some observers at the time believed that his actions during the treaty process caused the one Indian war fought in Washington territory, the Yakami War of 1855-56.

As more and more settlements developed, the traditional hunting and fishing areas of the Puget Sound tribes were appropriated by non-Natives and no longer available. Chief Seattle realized the futility of resisting this influx of settlers. He did everything he could to maintain friendly relations with the newcomers and tried to negotiate the best terms for his people.

TERMS OF THE TREATY

Governor Stevens was the chief negotiator at the Point Elliott Treaty as well as the other four treaties in the Washington Territory. The negotiations were conducted in English, translated into *Chinook* jargon (a shorthand language of about 300 words derived from French, English, and Indian languages) and then into two dialects of the Salish language. Language problems produced difficulties in translation, creating misunderstandings which persist to this day.

On January 22, 1855, the Point Elliott Treaty was ratified by more than twenty tribes from the Puget Sound area. By agreeing to the treaty, the participating tribes relinquished control of vast areas of ancestral land. The Suquamish tribe ceded 87,130 acres to the United States. They managed to keep only 7,486 acres.

The terms of the treaty stated that the tribes were to receive $150,000 as annuities and $15,000 for moving and resettlement expenses. They were granted all rights to fish at their ancestral grounds and to hunt and gather plant foods on all unclaimed lands. They were to maintain friendly relations with the non-Native people, not make war with other tribes except in self-defense, and not harbor lawbreakers. They were required to free all slaves and discontinue slavery. In exchange, "the United States was, under each treaty, to maintain for twenty years a carpenter, blacksmith and the necessary shops, a farmer, a physician with necessary medicines, and to support an agricultural and industrial school with proper instructors." (Eells, 1985, p. 28)

Some [of the people] *were in total agreement with him* [Chief Seattle] *as how things went, but there were others that didn't care for the way it was handled—whether it was blame Chief Seattle or whether they were blaming the White man for not keeping his promises, I don't know. But some of them thought that he gave in too easy.*
—Lawrence Webster

The old people thought they were each to be given a stove pipe hat of gold, similar to the one that President Lincoln wore, for moving to and living on the reservation. To this day it is unclear as to whether the Tribe received any money for the land they gave up. —Marilyn Jones

79

CHIEF SEATTLE'S SPEECH

Background for The Speech

Author's note: The first printed version of the speech was written by Dr. Smith and appeared in the October 29, 1887, edition of the *Seattle Sunday Star* newspaper in an article entitled, "Early Reminiscence Number 10, Scraps from a Diary."

According to Suquamish oral history, Chief Seattle gave his now-famous speech in December, 1854, during treaty negotiations with Isaac I. Stevens, the new governor and Commissioner of Indian Affairs for the Washington Territories. He was 67 or 68 at the time.

One of the people in attendance at the meeting was Dr. Henry Smith, who took extensive notes on Chief Seattle's speech. Dr. Smith had lived in the area for two years and is said to have learned Lushootseed, the primary indigenous language spoken throughout Puget Sound. Although the chief may have spoken some English, he delivered his speech in Lushootseed and not Chinook, which he refused to speak. According to the Suquamish, Dr. Smith spent several years visiting Chief Seattle, discussing the content of the speech so that Smith's recording would convey the chief's true meaning.

Several authors have felt free to create their own versions of the speech from Smith's original. The most widely circulated version of Chief Seattle's speech was written by Ted Perry, a theater arts professor and playwright at the University of Texas. Perry had heard an adaptation of the speech that had been delivered in an address by William Arrowsmith, a professor of classical literature at the University of Texas, during Earth Day in 1970. He asked Arrowsmith's permission to use the speech as the basis for a new fictitious speech which would serve as the narration for a film on pollution and ecology called *Home*. Without notifying Perry, the film's producers revised the text even further, adding phrases referring to God and the line, "I am a savage and do not understand." Also, without Perry's knowledge or permission, the film's credits stated that the script was a speech spoken by Chief Seattle and gave no acknowledgement that Perry had, in fact, written it. To promote the film, the producers sent out 18,000 posters with their version of Perry's script, claiming it was a speech given by Chief Seattle.

In a letter to the Book Publishing Company, Ted Perry states:

I left the project before post-production and awaited the film's showing on television many months later. When the film, *Home*, aired on ABC-TV in 1972, I was more than surprised to find that my 'written by' credit did not appear on the film. No one consulted with me about this change in credit, and I had not given my permission. When I contacted the producer, he wrote me that he thought the text would sound more authentic if the emphasis were placed on Chief Seattle. Objecting very strongly, I ended my work relationship with the producers, even though my contract called for me to write one more film for them. A few times I have written letters trying to correct the way the speech is presented, asking at the very least that the text be represented as 'inspired by' Seattle, but usually my letters are ignored.

Dr. Smith's version and Ted Perry's version are reprinted here.

RECOLLECTIONS OF DR. HENRY SMITH

When Governor Stevens first arrived in Seattle and told the Natives he had been appointed Commissioner of Indian Affairs for Washington Territory, they gave him a demonstrative reception in front of Dr. Maynard's office, near the waterfront on Main Street. The bay swarmed with canoes, and the shore was lined with a living mass of swaying, writhing, dusky humanity, until old Chief Seattle's trumpet-toned voice rolled over the immense multitude, like the startling reveille of a bass drum, when silence became as instantaneous and perfect as that which follows a clap of thunder from a clear sky.

The governor was then introduced to the Native multitude by Dr. Maynard, and at once commenced, in a conversational, plain, and straightforward style, an explanation of his mission among them, which is too well understood to require capitulation.

When he sat down, Chief Seattle arose with all the dignity of a senator, who carries the responsibilities of a great nation on his shoulders. Placing one hand on the governor's head and slowly pointing heavenward with the index finger of the other, he commenced his memorable address in solemn and impressive tones.

Other speakers followed but I took no notes. Governor Steven's reply was brief. He merely promised to meet them in general council on some future occasion to discuss the proposed treaty. Chief Seattle's promise to adhere to the treaty, should one be ratified, was observed to the letter, for he was ever the unswerving and faithful friend of the white man. (Smith, "Early Reminiscences," October, 1887)

CHIEF SEATTLE'S SPEECH
AS RECORDED BY DR. HENRY SMITH

Yonder sky that has wept tears of compassion on our fathers for centuries untold, and which to us, looks eternal, may change. Today it is fair, tomorrow it may be overcast with clouds. My words are like stars that never set. What Seattle says, the great chief, Washington can rely upon, with as much certainty as our pale-face brothers can rely upon the return of the seasons.

The son of the white chief says his father sends us greetings of friendship and good will. This is kind, for we know he has little need of our friendship in return, because his people are many. They are like the grass that covers the vast prairies, while my people are few, and resemble the scattering trees of a storm-swept plain. The great, and I presume also good, white chief sends us word that he wants to buy our land but is willing to allow us to reserve enough to live on comfortably. This indeed appears generous, for the red man no longer has rights that he need respect, and the offer may be wise, also, for we are no longer in need of a great country.

There was a time when our people covered the whole land, as the

The Indians in early times thought that Washington was still alive. They knew the name to be that of a president, and when they heard of the president at Washington they mistook the name of the city for the name of the reigning chief. They thought, also, that King George was still England's monarch, because the Hudson bay traders called themselves "King George men." This innocent deception the company was shrewd enough not to explain away for the Indians had more respect for them than they would have had, had they known England was ruled by a woman. (Grant, 1891)

waves of a wind-ruffled sea cover its shell-paved floor. But that time has long since passed away with the greatness of tribes now almost forgotten. I will not mourn over our untimely decay, nor reproach my pale-face brothers for hastening it, for we, too, may have been somewhat to blame.

When our young men grow angry at some real or imaginary wrong, and disfigure their faces with black paint, their hearts, also, are disfigured and turn black, and then their cruelty is relentless and knows no bounds, and our old men are not able to restrain them.

But let us hope that hostilities between the red-man and his pale-face brothers may never return. We would have everything to lose and nothing to gain. True it is, that revenge, with our young braves, is considered gain, even at the cost of their own lives, but old men who stay at home in times of war, and old women, who have sons to lose, know better.

Our great father Washington, for I presume he is now our father as well as yours, since George has moved his boundaries to the north; our great and good father, I say, sends us word by his son, who, no doubt, is a great chief among his people, that if we do as he desires, he will protect us. His brave armies will be to us a bristling wall of strength, and his great ships of war will fill our harbors so that our ancient enemies far to the northward, the Simsiams and Hydas will no longer frighten our women and old men. Then he will be our father and we will be his children.

Author's notes: Negotiations between the United States and Britain had resulted in the international boundary being moved north to the 49 parallel, thus giving the United States control over the Puget Sound region.

Governor Stevens had promised protection from aggressive tribes in the north if Chief Seattle's people would agree to the terms of the treaty.

But can this ever be? Your God loves your people and hates mine; he folds his strong arms lovingly around the white man and leads him as a father leads his infant son, but he has forsaken his red children; he makes your people wax strong every day, and soon they will fill the land; while my people are ebbing away like a fast-receding tide, that will never flow again. The white man's God cannot love his red children or he would protect them. They seem to be orphans and can look nowhere for help. How can we become brothers? How can your father become our father and bring us prosperity and awaken in us dreams of returning greatness?

Your God seems to us to be partial. He came to the white man. We never saw Him. We never even heard His voice. He gave the white man laws but He had no word for His red children whose teeming millions filled this vast continent as the stars fill the firmament. No, we are two distinct races and must ever remain so. There is little in common between us. The ashes of our ancestors are sacred and their final resting place is hallowed ground, while you wander away from the tombs of your fathers seemingly without regret. Your religion was written on tables of stone by the iron finger of an angry God, lest you might forget it. The red-man could never remember nor comprehend it.

Our religion is the traditions of our ancestors, the dreams of our old men, given them by the great Spirit, and the visions of our sachems, and is written in the hearts of our people.

Your dead cease to love you and the homes of their nativity as soon as they pass the portals of the tomb. They wander far off beyond the stars, are soon forgotten, and never return.

Our dead never forget the beautiful world that gave them being. They still love its winding rivers, its great mountains and its sequestered valleys, and they ever yearn in tenderest affection over the lonely hearted living and often return to visit and comfort them.

Day and night cannot dwell together. The red man has ever fled the approach of the white man, as the changing mists on the mountain side flee before the blazing morning sun.

However, your proposition seems a just one, and I think my folks will accept it and will retire to the reservation you offer them, and we will dwell apart and in peace, for the words of the great white chief seem to be the voice of nature speaking to my people out of the thick darkness that is fast gathering around them like a dense fog floating inward from a midnight sea. It matters but little where we pass the remainder of our days. They are not many.

The Indian's night promises to be dark. No bright star hovers about the horizon. Sad-voiced winds moan in the distance. Some grim Nemesis of our race is on the red man's trail, and wherever he goes he will still hear the sure approaching footsteps of the fell destroyer and prepare to meet his doom, as does the wounded doe that hears the approaching footsteps of the hunter. A few more moons, a few more winters and not one of all the mighty hosts that once filled this broad land or that now roam in fragmentary bands through these vast solitudes will remain to weep over the tombs of a people once as powerful and as hopeful as your own.

But why should we repine? Why should I murmur at the fate of my people? Tribes are made up of individuals and are no better than they. Men come and go like the waves of the sea. A tear, a tamanawus, a dirge, and they are gone from our longing eyes forever. Even the white man, whose God walked and talked with him, as friend to friend, is not exempt from the common destiny. We may be brothers after all. We shall see.

We will ponder your proposition, and when we have decided we will tell you. But should we accept it, I here and now make this first condition: That we will not be denied the privilege, without molestation, of visiting at will the graves of our ancestors and friends. Every part of this country is sacred to my people. Every hill-side, every valley, every plain and grove has been hallowed by some fond memory or sad experience of my tribe.

Even the rocks that seem to lie dumb as they swelter in the sun along the silent seashore in solemn grandeur thrill with memories of past events connected with the fate of my people, and the very dust under your feet responds more lovingly to our footsteps than to yours, because it is the ashes of our ancestors, and our bare feet are conscious of the sympathetic touch, for the soil is rich with the life of our kindred.

The sable braves, and fond mothers, and glad-hearted maidens, and the little children who lived and rejoiced here, and whose very names are now forgotten, still love these solitudes, and their deep fastnesses at eventide grow shadowy with the presence of dusky spirits. And when the last red man shall have perished from the earth and his memory among white man shall have become a myth, these shores shall swarm with the invisible dead of my tribe, and when your children's children shall think themselves alone in the field, the store, the shop, upon the highway or in the silence of the woods, they will not be alone. In all the earth there is no place dedicated to solitude. At night, when the streets of your cities and villages shall be silent, and you think them deserted, they will throng with the returning hosts that once filled and still love this beautiful land. The white man will never be alone. Let him be just and deal kindly with my people, for the dead are not altogether powerless.

THE SPEECH BY TED PERRY
INSPIRED BY CHIEF SEATTLE

Every part of this earth is sacred to my people. Every shining pine needle, every tender shore, every vapor in the dark woods, every clearing, and every humming insect are holy in the memory and experience of my people. The sap which courses through the trees carries the memories of the red man.

The white man's dead forget the country of their birth when they walk among the stars. Our dead never forget this beautiful earth, for it is the mother of the red men. Our dead always love and remember the earth's swift rivers, the silent footsteps of spring, the sparkling ripples on the surface of the ponds, the gaudy colors of the birds. We are a part of the earth and it is a part of us. The perfumed flowers are our sisters; the deer, the horse, the great condor, these are our brothers. The rocky crests, the juices in the meadows, the body heat of the pony, and man all belong to the same family.

So when the Great Chief in Washington sends word that he wishes to buy our land, he asks much of us. What Chief Seattle says, the Great Chief in Washington can count on as surely as our white brothers can count on the return of the seasons. My words are like the stars. They do not set.

Chief Washington also sends us words of friendship and goodwill. This is kind of him.

So we will consider your offer to buy our land. It will not be easy. This land is sacred to us. We take our pleasure in the woods and the dancing streams. The water that moves in the brooks is not water but the blood of our ancestors. If we sell you the land, you must remember that it is sacred to us, and forever teach your children that it is sacred. Each ghostly reflection in the clear water of the lakes tells of events and memories in the life of my people.

The water's gurgle is the voice of my father's father. The rivers are our brothers; they quench our thirst. The rivers, between the tender arms of their banks, carry our canoes where they will.

If we sell our land, you must remember, and teach your children, that the rivers are our brothers, and yours, and you must henceforth give the rivers the kindness you would give to any brother.

So Chief Seattle will consider the offer of Chief Washington. We will consider. The red man has always retreated before the advancing white man, as the mist on the mountain slopes runs before the morning sun. To us the ashes of our fathers are sacred. Their graves are holy ground, and so these hills, these trees. This portion of earth is consecrated to us.

The white man does not understand. One portion of land is the same to him as the next, for he is a wanderer who comes in the night and borrows from the land whatever he needs. The earth is not his brother, but his enemy, and when he has won the struggle, he moves on. He leaves his father's graves behind, and he does not care. He kidnaps the earth from his children. And he does not care. The father's graves and the children's birthright are forgotten by the white man, who treats his mother the earth and his brother the sky as things to be bought, plundered, and sold, like sheep, bread, or bright beads. In this way, the dogs of appetite will devour the rich earth and leave only a desert.

The white man is like a snake who eats his own tail in order to live. And the tail grows shorter and shorter. Our ways are different from your ways. We do not live well in your cities, which seem like so many black warts on the face of the earth. The sight of the white man's cities pains the eyes of the red man like the sunlight which stabs the eyes of one emerging from a dark cave. There is no place in the white man's cities quiet enough to hear the unfurling of leaves in Spring or the rustle of insects' wings. In the white man's cities, one is always trying to outrun an avalanche. The clatter only seems to pierce the ears. But what is there to living if a man cannot hear the lonely cry of the thrush or the arguments of the frogs around a pond at night?

But I am a red man and do not understand. I prefer the wind darting over the face of a pond and the smell of the wind itself, cleansed by a midday rain shower. The air is precious to the red man, for all things share the same breath — the beasts, the trees, and man, they are all of the same breath. The white man does not mind the foul air he breathes. Like a man in pain for many days, he is numb to the stench.

But if we sell our land, you must remember that the air is precious to us, and our trees, and the beasts. The wind gives man his first breath and receives his last sigh. And if we sell you our land, you will keep it apart and sacred, as a place where even the white man can go to taste a wind sweetened by meadow flowers.

So we will consider your offer to buy our land. If we decide to accept, I will here and now make one condition: the white man must treat the beasts of this land as his brothers.

I have heard stories of a thousand rotting buffaloes on the prairie, left by the white men who shot them from a passing train. I do not understand. For us, the beasts are our brothers, and we kill only to stay alive.

If we sell him this land, the white man must do the same, for the animals are our brothers. What is man without the beast? Even the earthworm keeps the earth soft for man to walk upon. If all the beasts were gone, men would die from great loneliness. For whatever happens to the beasts, happens to man for we are all of one breath. We will consider your offer to buy our land.

Do not send men asking us to decide more quickly. We will decide in our time. Should we accept, I here and now make this condition: we will never be denied the right to walk softly over the graves of our fathers, mothers, and friends, nor may the white man desecrate these graves.

The graves must always be open to the sunlight and the falling rain. Then the water will fall gently upon the green sprouts and seep slowly down to moisten the parched lips of our ancestors and quench their thirst.

If we sell this land to you, I will make now this condition: You must teach your children that the ground beneath their feet responds more loving-ly to our steps than to yours, because it is rich with the lives of our kin.

Teach your children what we have taught our children, that the earth is our mother. Whatever befalls the earth, befalls the sons of the earth. If men spit upon the ground, they spit upon themselves. This we know. The earth does not belong to the white man, the white man belongs to the earth. This we know.

All things are connected like the blood which unites our family. If we kill the snakes, the field mice will multiply and destroy our corn.

All things are connected. Whatever befalls the earth, befalls the sons and daughters of the earth. Man did not weave the web of life; he is merely a strand in it. Whatever he does to the web, he does to himself.

No, day and night cannot live together. We will consider your offer.

What is it that the white man wishes to buy, my people ask me? The idea is strange to us. How can you buy or sell the sky, the warmth of the land, the swiftness of the antelope? How can we sell these things to you and how can you buy them?

Is the earth yours to do with as you will, merely because the red man signs a piece of paper and gives it to the white man? If we do not own the freshness of the air and the sparkle of the water, how can you buy them from us? Can you buy back the buffalo, once the last one has died?

But we will consider your offer. In his passing moment of strength, the white man thinks that he is a god who can treat his mother (the earth), the rivers (which are his sisters), and his red brothers, as he wishes. But the man who would buy and sell his mother, his brothers, and sisters would also burn his children to keep himself warm.

So we will consider your offer to buy our land. Day and night cannot live together. Your offer seems fair, and I think my people will accept it and go to the reservation you have for them. We will live apart, and in peace.

Tribes are made of men, nothing more. Men come and go, like the waves of the sea. The whites too shall pass; perhaps sooner than all other tribes. Continuing to contaminate his own bed, the white man will one night suffocate in his own filth.

But in his perishing the white man will shine brightly, fired by the strength of the god who brought him to this land and for some special purpose gave him dominion over this land. That destiny is a mystery to us, for we do not understand what living becomes when the buffalo are all slaughtered, the wild horses all tamed, the secret corners of the forest are heavy with the scent of many men, and the view of the ripe hills blotted by talking wires.

Where is the thicket? Gone. Where is the eagle? Gone. And what is it to say goodbye to the swift pony and the hunt? The end of living and the beginning of survival.

The white man's god gave him dominion over the beasts, the woods, and the red man, for some special purpose, but that destiny is a mystery to the red man. We might understand if we knew what it was that the white man dreams, what hopes he describes to children on long winter nights, what visions he burns onto their eyes so that they will wish for tomorrow. The white man's dreams are hidden from us. And because they are hidden, we will go our own way.

So we will consider your offer to buy our land. If we agree, it will be to secure the reservation you have promised. There, perhaps, we may live out our brief days as we wish. There is little in common between us.

If we sell you our land, it will be filled with the bold young men, the warm breasted mothers, the sharp-minded women, and the little children who once lived and were happy here.

Your dead go to walk among the stars, but our dead return to the earth they love. The white man will never be alone unless, in some distant day, he destroys the mountains, the trees, the rivers, and the air. If the earth should come to that, and the spirits of our dead, who love the earth, no longer wish to return and visit their beloved, then in that noon glare that pierces the eyes, the white man will walk his desert in great loneliness.

LIFE AFTER THE TREATY

YAKIMA WAR

Chief Seattle was a peace chief. We had one, Chief Kitsap, they kinda' outlawed, because he wouldn't agree with the treaty. He was a war chief.

Big John was for war but he was in agreement with Chief Seattle on this, from what I could understand, heard when I was a youngster.

—Lawrence Webster

The language difficulties and the speediness of the negotiations created confusion among tribal leaders as to what they agreed to. This, along with other issues, ultimately led to an uprising, waged by some tribes in the area, called the Yakima War of 1855-56. The area of hostilities extended from southern Oregon near the Rogue River north to the Yakima River in Washington, and from Puget Sound to the western side of the Cascade mountains.

A number of Puget Sound tribes took part, including the Duwamish, Puyallups, Nisquallies, and the White River people. They were led by the chiefs Leshi, Quiemuth, Kitsay, Nelson, and Stehi. During the hostilities, several families on the White River were massacred and the town of Seattle was attacked and much of it burned. Fighting continued into the beginning of 1856 but was soon over. The Indians had no experience waging a prolong war and were poorly organized.

The waring bands were soon driven into the Cascade Mountains where they were killed or captured. Their effort to drive out the settlers was over. True to his word, Chief Seattle kept his people out of the war and even warned settlers when danger was near. He is said to have told Chief Leshi not to attack the town of Seattle.

The United States Congress took four years to ratify the Point Elliott Treaty, during which time many of the agreements were violated and more Native holdings lost. Three years after the treaty, Chief Seattle pleaded his people's case to an American official:

> I fear that we are forgotten or that we are to be cheated out of our land. . . . I have been very poor and hungry all winter and am very sick now. In a little while I will die. I should like to be paid for my lands before I die. Many of my people died during the cold winter without getting their pay . . . We are ashamed when we think of the Puyallups, as they have now got their papers. They fought against the whites wiliest we, who have never been angry with them, get nothing. (Costello, 1895)

In a letter, George Gibbs, an official present at most of the treaty signings in Washington Territory writes:

> Difficulty will arise from the non-fulfillment of the treaties with the friendly tribes. The treaty with the Nisquallies [and others], who took up arms, was the only one ratified, and of course they will receive their annuities; while the Lower Sound tribes, who have remained peaceable, and have been compelled to suffer great through necessary inconvenience, remain neglected. Whether the treaties are good or not, they ought to be ratified, or at least provision made by law to pay their annuities as promised. (Lane & Lane, *The Treaties of Puget Sound 1854-55*)

After the treaty, the tribes of Puget Sound became increasingly impoverished and in control of a fraction of the land and resources they once had. Although the Treaty of Point Elliott provided that the Port Madison Reservation be held "in trust" for the tribe by the federal government, pressure rapidly increased for sale of these lands. Logging companies were interested in the timber, and entrepreneurs looking for investment property were

But I heard a lot of 'em say afterwards that they shouldn't 'a signed, because they never got paid for the land they gave away. And right up until this century, like old Jenny Davis, and Annie Rogers, when they died they were still lookin' for their two buckets a' gold that was promised to 'em.

—Lawrence Webster

103

attracted to the reservation's proximity to Seattle and the pleasant surroundings. Therefore, almost immediately after land was allotted, the Indian-owned property began to diminish.

Reservation Life

Although the Point Elliott Treaty gave the Suquamish a reservation of their own to live on, they continued to suffer disruption of their culture and the loss of land to white settlers and the United States government.

The beginning of reservation life marked a significant transition in Suquamish history. Federal agents were assigned to take charge of the reservation, despite the existence of strong tribal leadership. In the decades following the Treaty of 1855, the federal government made gradual attempts to put an end to the traditions and communal lifestyle of the Suquamish people. Certain ceremonies and religious practices were outlawed at this time. Additionally, in the 1870s the acting federal agent at Port Madison ordered the burning of Old Man House at Agate Pass, the physical and spiritual heart of the Suquamish community.

During the following years, families continued to live in the village surrounding this site. At the turn of the century, the village included over thirty-five homes, a Catholic church, a schoolhouse, smokehouse, and several orchards. Village life was further disrupted when, in 1905, the United States War Department acquired nearly fifty acres of this land for a proposed military post. Houses were uprooted, as were the schoolhouse and church. Those having to move were paid twenty-four dollars apiece. Each family was to move to an individual parcel of land, or allotment, on the reservation. Suquamish leaders, concerned for their traditional homeland and the dispersal of their people, agreed to move from the village and, according to tribal elders, with the understanding that the property would return to the tribe if no longer needed for military purposes. Although a military post was never established, the land did not return to tribal possession.

From 1886 to 1910, land allotments were made on the reservation according to a provision in the Point Elliott Treaty. This action paralleled federal policy aimed at creating independent family farmsteads. The government hoped to replace traditional ways with those of white society by encouraging ownership of private land and farming among Indians. Yet the Suquamish were able to farm very little, as the land was poorly suited for such purposes, maintaining instead their fishing and hunting lifestyle. An allotment owner was expected to clear, develop, and otherwise "improve" his land or risk losing it. These allotments were scattered throughout the reservation, often covered by dense forests far from the shore, a primary source of food.

Some families homesteaded lands off the reservation because an insufficient number of allotments were created. Others chose to remain in traditional off-reservation villages and tried to acquire land through homesteading.

Although some Indians chose to sell their land, much was sold without the owner's consent by federal agents who deemed the Indian owner "noncompetent" if, for example, they could not speak English or lacked a monetary income. (The Suquamish Museum, 1985)

Terms of the treaty are being argued over to this day, more than 130 years later!

107

INDIAN BOARDING SCHOOLS

I was away for about eight years going to school. And that life span of eight years—a lot of changes took place. —Lawrence Webster

I wouldn't even notice I'd say something in Indian, and then the teacher'd come along with his ruler and hit me on the hand, "You talk English." —Ethel Sam

It [Tulalip] *was like a military school. You lined up and marched to almost everything you did. And boy, you toed the mark . . . all the little kids, right down to the smallest one. They had companies— Company A and B. You lined up . . . by bugle calls, just like the Army . . . and then they had marching competition—the girls and boys. And by God, we couldn't beat those girls.*
—Woody Loughrey

The original intent of missionaries in establishing boarding schools was to teach Native people the skills they would need to survive in the white society. But these schools became a tool of cultural destruction and oppression by the United States and caused untold hardships on family life.

From the 1880s through the 1920s, the federal government made an intensive effort to assimilate Indian people into white society by attempting to eliminate the cultural heritage of Indian youth, and replace it with non-Native values. Thus began the policy of removing children from their families and sending them to Indian boarding schools off their reservations. Many industrial schools were established to supplement or replace those boarding schools already started by missionaries.

Together with children from other tribes across the nation, Suquamish children attended schools near Tacoma and Everett in Washington, as well as schools in Oregon and California. Today tribal elders remember the schools with mixed feelings. Some feel that the strict discipline, academic studies, and job skills helped prepare them for later life. Yet many students, particularly women, expecting to receive a useful education found themselves instead serving an economic function in the daily operation and maintenance of the schools.

Being removed from their home communities and prohibited from practicing cultural traditions was a great hardship. Tragedy struck several schools in western Washington when epidemics of whooping cough, measles, and other communicable diseases took the lives of countless children, who were concentrated together in one place and had no natural immunity to such diseases of the white man. By the late twenties, a movement had begun to reform Indian education. (The Suquamish Museum, 1985)

THE SUQUAMISH TRIBE

SUQUAMISH
PLACE OF CLEAR SALT WATER

The Port Madison Indian Reservation was established by the Point Elliott Treaty of 1854, in which the Suquamish and several other tribes were given exclusive use of 7,486 acres of land in Kitsap County. Located on the Kitsap Peninsula, it is a beautiful section of the county and lies west across Puget Sound from the present day city of Seattle. Also, under terms of the treaty, the Suquamish and other tribes were allowed continued use of areas around the reservation. As a result, a large portion of the northeastern tip of the Olympic Peninsula, including most of Kitsap County, all of Puget Sound, and waters north to Canada, were established as "Usual and Accustomed Areas" of the tribe for fishing, hunting, and gathering, including digging clams.

In 1855 the Suquamish tribe was officially recognized as a sovereign nation by the United States. Today the seat of government is located at the Suquamish Tribal Center near the village of Suquamish within the Port Madison Indian Reservation.

GOVERNMENT

As of the year 2000, there were 1,000 registered members of the Suquamish tribe, and they make up what is called the Suquamish General Council. A seven-member Tribal Council is elected by voting age members of the General Council and operates under a constitution and by-laws. They take care of the business of the tribe and direct the work of a 145 person staff with an annual budget of over four million dollars.

The Tribal Center, built in 1979, is where all government and other official tribal activities happen. Located here are the offices for administration, fisheries, natural resources, community development, finance, human services, maintenance, cultural resources, legal and personnel, and self-governance. Also located here is the tribal council meeting room and the Suquamish Museum.

The tribe, being a sovereign nation, enacts their own laws and enforces them through their public safety department. Infractions are dealt with in their court system or through a mediation process. The tribe operates a preschool and a daycare center located in the Tribal Center, as well as an elder's council and a youth council that works with the Tribal Council.

Before Euro-American contact the Suquamish had seven chiefs, so today there are seven council members to reflect to old tradition.

—Marilyn Jones

Museum

In 1983, the Suquamish Museum was established to "preserve, protect, and exhibit tribal culture, history, and artifacts." Over 10,000 visitors a year from all parts of the world come to the museum. The exhibits "The Eyes of Chief Seattle" and "Old Man House: the People and Their Way of Life at D'Suq'Wub" and the award-winning media productions *Come Forth Laughing: Voices of the Suquamish People* and *Waterborne: Gift of the Indian Canoe* are helping people gain a better understanding of the lives and experiences of the Native culture of northwest Washington.

The Lushootseed language, the indigenous language of Puget Sound, is close to extinction. As of the year 2000, there were fewer than sixty native speakers left alive. In an effort to preserve the language, the Suquamish are teaching their children the language in their preschool at the Suquamish Early Learning Center. They are developing a phonetic alphabet and dictionary and writing software to build a language computer. And once more, Suquamish children are being named in the Lushootseed language. On another front, there are efforts by a group called the Native American Multimedia Project to acquire grants to preserve the Lushootseed language and other languages in the area. Let's hope they are successful.

The museum that we have now will help the younger people see who was ahead of them. —Lawrence Webster

CHIEF SEATTLE DAYS

Each year since 1911, the Suquamish tribe has held a celebration called "Chief Seattle Days." It's a public celebration of culture and heritage held in honor of their famous leader and features a memorial service held at Chief Seattle's grave site. People from all over the region come to this three-day event, held in the third weekend of August. Other activities include a fishing derby, salmon and clam bake, canoe races, traditional songs, drumming, and story-telling. Crafts and art from the region are displayed and sold. In addition, a powwow is held with dancers competing for prize money. Baseball was a big part of the celebration in the early years, and a game is usually held between area teams. A highlight of the event is the royalty pageant during which a Miss Chief Seattle Days Princess is chosen to represent the tribe for a year.

[In] 1911 they had one, brought in quite a few people from Seattle, put on the Seattle Day Celebration. Well, that seemed to draw 'em a little closer together because before they had that celebration, there was very little association between the non-Indian and the Indian.

—Lawrence Webster

CASINO

Like other sovereign tribal nations, the Suquamish operate a gambling casino on their reservation. The roulette wheels began turning December, 1995. The casino has created jobs in an area of high unemployment and has begun to make money for the tribe. When the facility is up to full capacity, they will operate 12,870 electronic gaming devices with 85% of the proceeds going to the tribe.

As stated in Initiative 671 of the State of Washington: "Gaming facilities

can assist tribes in restoring their economies and improve their general wel-
fare by providing employment and economic development opportunities and
revenue for improved education, health care, social services, fisheries, and
natural resource protection and enhancement, and public safety services."

CONCLUSION

Puget Sound was the main source of food before Euro-American contact and is still an important source of livelihood for many Native people in this region. Tribal leaders continue to argue in the courts for fishing and hunting rights granted in the Point Elliott Treaty of 1854. In 1974, a federal court awarded tribal members the right to fifty percent of the local salmon catch in their "usual and accustomed" areas. Another court ruling in 1995 gave the sixteen tribes of Puget Sound the right to fifty percent of local shellfish. Hunting rights were upheld in State v. Buchanan, August, 1997. In that case the Washington State Court of Appeals upheld the treaty right for tribal members to hunt on opened and unclaimed land anywhere in the state.

Salmon runs of today have been reduced as much as ninety percent from overfishing by commercial interests and the disruptive effects of dams and reservoirs. In an effort to ensure the salmon's survival, the Suquamish tribe operates a fish hatchery and stocks Agate Pass and other areas. Each year the tribe releases over five million fish into the Puget Sound water system. After release, the young fish swim out to sea to feed and mature. A small percentage survive and eighteen months later return to be harvested by grateful Native fishermen.

The timber and marine resources of this region have been heavily harvested since ownership passed out of Native hands and by 1920 were much depleted. But conservation efforts begun in the 1970s are beginning to reverse the decline. The sea otter, hunted close to extinction, has been reintroduced and is now flourishing. Today this area is home to the densest population of bald eagles in the lower 48 states. The ecosystem seems to be recovering, but there is much more that needs to be done.

Today, because of federal policies after the Point Elliott Treaty, a large percentage of reservation lands are owned by non-Indian residents. A major goal for the tribe has been to purchase land on the Port Madison Reservation for the benefit of the Suquamish community. The establishment of a tribal housing development department has enabled many Suquamish people to move back to the reservation.

The future looks promising for the Suquamish people of Puget Sound. Because of Chief Seattle's efforts, the tribe controls a large, secure land base. After decades of decline, their population is growing. Their dedicated leaders have a strong sense of tribal identity and are wise to the ways of the modern world. And they work hard for the good of the people. Add to this the potential for a significant revenue stream from casino operations and they seem to have a great formula for success. All the best to the Suquamish people.

The Suquamish can be contacted at:

The Suquamish Tribe
P.O. Box 498
Suquamish, WA 98392-0498
Phone: 360-598-3311
Fax: 360-598-6295
http://www.suquamish.nsn.us

The Suquamish Museum
P.O. Box 490
Suquamish, WA 98392-0498
Phone: 360-598-3111 ext. 422

SELECTED BIBLIOGRAPHY

Bagley, Clarence B. 1916. *History of Seattle: From the Earliest Settlements to the Present Time.* Vol. 1. Chicago: The S. J. Clark Publishing Company.

------*Bagley's Scrapbook*, No. 5. Special Collections, Washington State University, Seattle, Washington.

Coombs, S. F. "Good Chief Seattle, How A Young Warrior Became Ruler of Many Tribes." *Post-Intelligencer*, March 26, 1893.

Costello, J. A. 1895. *The Siwash, Their Life, Legends, and Tales: Puget Sound and Pacific Northwest.* Seattle: The Calvert Company.

Curtis, Edward S. 1913. *The North American Indians Vol. 9: Salishan Tribes of the Coast, The Chimakum, The Quiliute, and The Willapa.* Norwood: Limpton Press.

Eells, Myron. 1985. *The Indians of Puget Sound: The Notebooks of Myron Eells.* Edited by George P. Castile. Seattle: University of Washington Press.

Furtwangler, Albert. 1997. *Answering Chief Seattle.* Seattle & London: University of Washington Press.

Giffford, Eli. *The Many Speeches of Seathl: The Manipulation of The Record on Behalf of Religious, Political, and Environmental Causes,* master's thesis, Sonoma State University, Sonoma, 1998.

Giffford, Eli & Robert Michael Cook. 1992. *How Can One Sell the Air?: Chief Seattle's Vision.* Summertown: Book Publishing Company.

Grant, Frederick James. 1891. *History of Seattle, Washington.* New York: American Publishing and Engraving Company.

Lane, Robert B. & Barbara Lane. *The Treaties of Puget Sound 1854-55.* The Fourth World Documentation Project.

Lincoln, Leslie. 1991. *Coast Salish Canoes*. Seattle: Center for Wooden Boats.

Nunis, Doyce B., Jr. Editor. 1993. *From Mexican Days to the Gold Rush: Memoirs of James W. Marshall and Edward G. Buffum Who Grew Up with California*. Chicago: R.R. Donnelley and Sons Company.

Paterek, Josephine. 1994. *Encyclopedia of American Indian Costume*. New York: W.W. Norton & Company.

Perry, Ted. 1970. *Home*. Movie script for television series produced by Southern Baptist's Radio and Television Commission.

Perry, Ted to Michael Cook, Middlebury, Vermont, 30 October, 1992, Book Publishing Company: Summertown, Tennessee.

Point Elliott Treaty. National Archives, Washington, D.C.

Richards, Kent D. 1993. *Isaac I. Stevens: Young Man in a Hurry*. Reprint, Pullman: Washington State University Press.

Smith, Henry. 1887. "Scraps from a Diary - Chief Seattle - A Gentleman by Instinct - His Native Eloquence." *The Seattle Sunday Star*, October 29.

Suquamish Tribal Oral History Project, Suquamish Tribal Archives, Suquamish Museum. Suquamish, Washington.

The Suquamish Museum. 1985. *The Eyes of Chief Seattle*. Seattle: The Suquamish Museum.

U. S. Department of Interior, Bureau of Indian Affairs, *Indian Tribes West of the Cascades*, by Isaac I. Stevens. Open-file report, Annual Report of the Office of Indian Affairs, 453. Washington, D.C., 1854.

Look for these other Native American titles at your local book store or order from:
Book Publishing Co.
P.O. Box 99
Summertown, TN 38483
800-695-2241
Please add
$3.50 per book for shipping

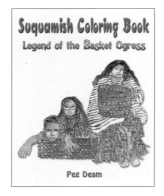

$4.95

$6.95

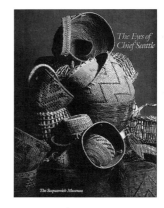

$16.95

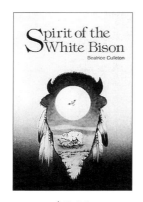

$5.95

$5.95

$16.95

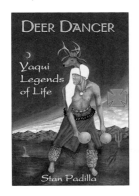

$11.95

$7.95

$9.95

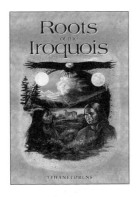

$9.95

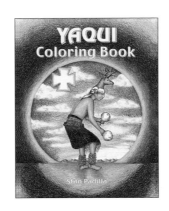

$4.95

$9.95